LOVING *the* CHAMPION

LOVING *the* CHAMPION

Parenting Young Golf Champions

JORGE GOMEZ

BALBOA.
PRESS
A DIVISION OF HAY HOUSE

Balboa Press books may be ordered through booksellers or by contacting:

Balboa Press
A Division of Hay House
1663 Liberty Drive
Bloomington, IN 47403
www.balboapress.com
1-(877) 407-4847

Because of the dynamic nature of the Internet, any web addresses or links contained in this book may have changed since publication and may no longer be valid. The views expressed in this work are solely those of the author and do not necessarily reflect the views of the publisher, and the publisher hereby disclaims any responsibility for them.

The author of this book does not dispense medical advice or prescribe the use of any technique as a form of treatment for physical, emotional, or medical problems without the advice of a physician, either directly or indirectly. The intent of the author is only to offer information of a general nature to help you in your quest for emotional and spiritual well-being. In the event you use any of the information in this book for yourself, which is your constitutional right, the author and the publisher assume no responsibility for your actions.

Any people depicted in stock imagery provided by Thinkstock are models, and such images are being used for illustrative purposes only. Certain stock imagery © Thinkstock.

Printed in the United States of America

ISBN: 978-1-4525-6819-5 (sc)
ISBN: 978-1-4525-6820-1 (e)

Balboa Press rev. date: 2/7/2013

TABLE OF CONTENTS

ACKNOWLEDGEMENTS

I want to extend my thanks to my great teachers, the children and teenagers, whom I have had the pleasure of teaching over the years, and who, despite their young age, have been able to teach me so much. Their happy faces, innocent and pure, have given me experiences, some wonderful, and some less so, which, together, have taught me so many important lessons.

I would also like to thank my current and former adult students, who by sharing their experiences, have also taught me so many things.

To the mothers and fathers who have trusted me over the years, as we work together for the wellbeing of their champions.

To Anna Vaubel, for making this translation to english in a beautiful and impressive way.

To my kindred spirit, Jas, who, thanks to her amazing

soul, has helped me stay positive and motivated throughout my life, learning the importance of the word, that cosmic vibration that we all are and forever will be.

To my brothers; Juan, who has always been by my side as we shared many amazing experiences together, and Pedro, who, at his young age, has gone through experiences that have taught me to always follow your dreams despite the obstacles/opportunities that life presents.

To my father, Pedro, for having taught me how to be a player of the great sport of golf throughout my life, and for his discipline, which although sometimes overzealous, has taught me many lessons, both positive and negative.

To Andrea, she tolerates and accepts me in my teenage years and for teaching me what unconditional love is.

To Esther, my great life teacher, who has taught me to distinguish what I WANT from what I don't want and for being there at my side on the good and bad times.

To my own champion, Jorge, who has shown me what it means to be on the other side of the coin, as a father, friend, child and partner for life. Thank you for your authenticity, sincerity, affection and love.

And to my mother, Maite, who taught me through her unconditional love, that if you want to, you can. To love and to forgive, despite the physical distance. I know you are with Juan and me forever, guiding us from a higher place to help others.

Om Namah Shivaya.

Jorge

Prologue

Loving the Champion was written with love, and its purpose is to share experiences and wisdom with the parents of amazing little champions in order to help guide them in supporting their champions in a mindful way towards realizing their dreams.

Jorge is always PRESENT, radiating a simple, natural and authentic nature, spontaneously helping his students and friends to express themselves, to be authentic and to achieve self-realization.

In this wonderful book, Jorge guides us through the different stages of our Champions' lives, and he suggests a path that will help us help them to reach their goals and be triumphant.

In simple and clear terms, he also addresses "the purpose" of golf and what it means to "win".

Day by day, with amazing talent and skill, Jorge

magically customizes and shares his knowledge in a personalized way.

In other words, he adapts his techniques to each student's needs, and focuses on their personal growth, with a creative and fun approach.

This book includes real-life experiences that serve as lessons to be learned.

With a heartfelt smile, I thank you, Jorge, for this treasure... Loving the Champion.

Jas.

Introduction

This book has been written as a result of my experiences over the years as a junior golf instructor. Thanks to these varied experiences, happy, sad, sentimental, bitter, tough, embarrassing, and others, I have filled its pages with words full of love and knowledge.

Over time, I have helped families understand the process that their Champions go though in a sport such as golf, but in truth, it could be any sport. At times, I have cried out of happiness upon seeing one of these champions realize his or her dreams. Seeing the fruitful results of their efforts is the one of the best satisfactions that life has given me. Additionally, I have learned how important it is to enjoy the ride.

Looking back, I realize how much work, fun, learning and love I have experienced with each champion, each one with his own issues: fears, mental blocks, harmful attitudes, etc. Each champion is a unique individual.

Many people have helped me along the way and now, I want to help them; what you give, you get, and if I help people, people help me, if I give a hug, a get one back.

This book has been written with simple, everyday language, in an upbeat and friendly tone. Forget about complicated words and terms. Life is simple, easy and joyful.

If this book is in your hands here and now, believe me it is because *it* chose *you*. There are important topics here that will help you reaffirm or modify the way you support your champions.

This book is for parents who share the road with their champions. Whenever I refer to your champion, I am referring to your son *or* daughter.

As parents, we only want the well-being of our champions. We want them to have a full life, to be safe and positive, to meet their goals, and to be happy and healthy.

In order to support our champions towards this end, as parents, we need to know the best way to help them reach personal, professional and spiritual glory.

We need to understand them and support them mentally, spiritually and materially, while at the same time searching for balance so that our champions become honorable, gracious, compassionate and loving individuals, who help their fellow human being, who love themselves so they can love others, who are understanding, and who are patient with themselves and those around them.

I will also explain clearly the different stages, based on their age, of your champions' lives. I will discuss the role that you play, as parents, the role of the golf coach and other trainers, the purpose of a game, what it means to win, and the experiences of other champions, all in a friendly and fun way, always focused on understanding and helping our young champions to realize their goals and dreams.

Enjoy this book. It was created with love, joy, affection and humor.

Jorge.

AGES AND STAGES OF
YOUR CHAMPIONS

A S YOUR CHAMPIONS GROW AND evolve, it is important that you be familiar with each of the different stages of their lives in order to be able to guide them effectively. Knowing what to do at each age will allow you to help your champions achieve their goals with a clear, open, and healthy mind.

As parents of champions, we must guide and support them, but we mustn't forget that we, too, have an inner child, and that our champions teach us to be authentic, natural, and unique and to be excited about the most beautiful things in life; a tree, the clouds, the sky, a butterfly, running in a field with the wind in our faces. Is there anything more wonderful for the soul?

Remember to let out your inner child as often as you blink; only then can we be authentic, natural, and loving parents.

CHAMPIONS FROM 0 TO 7 YEARS OLD

WHEN CHAMPIONS ARE BORN, THEY are pure, innocent, and open to learning and new experiences. During this stage, it is important that your champions feel free to be themselves. Just to BE.

As parents, we must provide them with all the basics, including love and affection, hugs and kisses, and encouraging words in a calm and friendly tone of voice.

Nourishment. Champions delight in nourishment from the mother's breast. It reminds them of when they were in the womb, that loving contact when champions connect to their mothers to nurse and feel their warmth. If a mother cannot breastfeed, I recommend that she bottle feed her champion as if she were breast feeding him, cuddling with him so that he feels the same comforting warmth and affection.

Cleanliness. It is important that your champions be

kept clean and neat so that they feel well taken care of, so remember to check them often to make sure they are comfortable.

Love. Champions need to feel loved, so give them plenty of hugs and kisses, play with them often, and give them quality time.

By fulfilling these three basic needs, your champions will begin to feel they are just that, Champions!

They will grow up with a strong sense of self-esteem, healthy and confident in themselves and in their abilities.

When it comes to golf during this stage, it is important that champions understand that it's just a game, and I ask you, how do we play a game? Well, by having fun! They need to know that they are going to play golf *for fun*. They are going to run, express themselves, and be in contact with nature, which is so essential these days.

Your champion may be between 3 and 7 years old, a time when many of us introduce our champions to the beautiful sport of golf.

When parents ask me to give golf lessons to champions of this age, I say sure, and tell them that the class will last approximately thirty minutes. During this stage, a champion's ability to concentrate is short, maximum seven or ten minutes per activity, so I tell them, "Sure, and in our class, we have *fun*." I want the champions to understand that the GAME is FUN, so I bring out my inner-child, and we have FUN! How? That's easy! We run, we say silly things, we color the golf balls, and we play with one of their toys, helping me to teach them game strategy. YES, with their toys! We look at the ants on the golf course, the flowers, the clouds, and they teach me to be a kid again. And I teach them to have FUN on the golf course. This is how champions begin to associate GOLF with FUN.

It is also important that your golf instructor learn to use children's language: easy, practical, and with few words, so that your champion can learn faster.

One question that comes up often is, "When can our champions begin playing tournaments? How will you know when they are ready?" The answer is easy.

When they ask to.

As I said before, as parents, we introduce our champions to golf, we teach them to have fun, some basic techniques, the basic rules of the game, and we briefly mention tournaments.

When your champions *ask* to participate in a tournament, that is the time to support them to PLAY in a tournament…and I do mean PLAY, ok?

At this time, you can begin teaching them about tournaments, what they are, and why people play them. Remember that your champions are only about seven at this stage, and they need to understand that a tournament is an event where many children, friends and fellow golfers come together to PLAY, and the one who hits the least number of shots gets first place, and so on, but the objective is to PLAY and have FUN.

Later on, we will talk about what it means "to win."

At this stage, champions need to develop various physical abilities, that is, they need to play a range of sports in order to develop their skills in movement, coordination, team sports, water sports, etc.

It's fairly common that at some point after starting to play golf, your champions turn around and say to you, "Mom (Dad), I don't want to play golf anymore," or "I don't want to play golf today." So then, remembering that this is the freedom stage, we tell them fine, that we understand and support their decision. Then, faster than a cricket can jump, your champions come back to ask if they can play golf again, assuming that the process up until now has been FUN. Why wouldn't you want to do something all the time if you know it's going to be FUN?

If they don't ask to play golf again, you should talk to them and ask them to tell you why they don't want to play golf, so that you can help them in an understanding, affectionate and loving manner, and maybe by simply changing a few attitudes, they can PLAY golf and have FUN again.

If they still don't want to play golf, well, that's easy. Your champions will still be champions, but in another sport or another area in life in which they choose. We must accept it.

CHAMPIONS BETWEEN 7 AND 14 YEARS OLD

W E CONTINUE SUPPORTING OUR CHAMPIONS. At this stage, our champions are more aware of what they really want, a process that depends on their maturity level. As is always the case, this stage follows an earlier process and is the beginning of a new process.

During this stage, it is important to teach your champions good habits, such as healthy eating habits. They should learn and understand why it is important to eat fruits and vegetables, pastas, etc. as well as to hydrate with water, and how and when to hydrate with energy drinks. They should also learn about rest, how many hours of sleep they need in order to allow their bodies to create the substances necessary for their proper physical, hormonal and mental development. They should also have a consistent exercise routine to keep their bodies (their temples) in good shape, strong and healthy. Parents should know how they get along with their fellow golfers and which ones they have things in common with and which ones they don't.

From a sports perspective, we can begin to intelligently introduce our champions deeper into the world of golf through more tournaments, more intense training, by setting concrete and specific goals, and by motivating them with emotional prizes or even small gifts. Notice, I did say, "small."

When you champions begin adolescence, as early as twelve years old, it is important to remember that they will experience hormonal changes, physical changes, mental changes, and a bit of everything, just as we did when we were that age. They will begin to be interested in the opposite sex, and begin to have new interests, but just remember that everything will be ok, it's a process and we, as parents, are there to help them through it.

This is the age when your champions most need your support and understanding, so that they will always be by your side. Remember that forbidden things always cause the most temptation. It has always been that way, and today's marketing makes it worse.

During this stage, it's as if we have a rubber band connected to our champions, which stretches and retracts depending on how hard we pull on it. There are times when we need to be yielding, and other times when we need to pull gently and lovingly on the rubber band, keeping in mind that if we pull too hard, it might break, and if it breaks, your champions will feel alone and misunderstood, which, believe me, is not a good feeling. So what better than to focus on what we really want, which is to have a pleasant, harmonious, genuine, respectful and honest relationship with our champions.

Remember that everyone needs their own space and time for themselves, so please make sure that you give some to your champions. They need it!

During this stage, if your champions are committed to golf and practice and play tournaments regularly, I recommend that they take an occasional break from golf. When I was young, I always took a two or three-week vacation, during which I didn't even put on a golf shirt, much less touch a club. This is healthy for the mind and as well as to break up the monotony, so that when your champions come back to golf, they come back with renewed energy.

CHAMPIONS FROM
14 TO 21 YEARS OLD

W E CONTINUE ALONG THE PROCESS of your champions, and as I mentioned earlier, each new process builds on the last one and finally gives way to a new one. This is the stage when your champion decides to dedicate his life, or at least a large portion of his life, to golf.

This stage is especially important, because what they choose to do during these years will mark their lives.

There are various options during this stage, from playing professionally or getting a college golf scholarship to study in another part of the world, to learning how to instruct others to play golf, etc.

Champions need to focus on their purpose, their personal dreams. They also need to form a training group that includes a golf coach, a nutritionist, a physical trainer, a mental trainer, etc. A well-formed group will help ensure the success of your champions. Later on, we will discuss in more detail the role of each member of this training group.

However, I understand that this is expensive. These days, there are people who want to help and who have general knowledge of all of these areas, and this can be an excellent alternative. I have seen some individuals who have proven excellent results. Their ability to develop a good relationship with the champions and their parents in all aspects creates a great combination.

For those interested in getting a college scholarship, it is important that by age fifteen, they already have or are beginning to have international exposure, meaning that they play international tournaments. These tournaments can be selected with the help of the golf coach, taking into consideration which tournaments are the best match to the champions' game, i.e., whether they prefer to play at sea level or high-altitude, on a windy or still day, in hot or cold weather, in the rain or in the sun, short courses or long courses, and other factors to be considered when choosing tournaments. Additionally, if your champions intend to study abroad, they will need to know which university coaches will be at which tournaments. There are certain tournaments that are especially popular among university coaches to choose their future champions.

It is especially important that we remain close to our champions during this stage; I have seen many great champions lose their way, change directions, and take different roads, diverting from their original goal, their final objective. This is why we need to be more empathetic with them. Remember when they were little, how we used to put on our five-year-old hat? In the same way, we now must put on our fifteen-year-old hat, and so forth and so on with each stage. We need to understand them, to lead them in a calm, loving, and kind way to the clouds that will take them to their dreams.

Additionally, they will be experimenting with the opposite sex during this stage, a time when their sexuality is being defined. We need to be alert and open-eyed in order to guide them with affection towards the road to success, health, happiness and love.

As is true for all processes, your champions need to learn for themselves. As parents, we can guide them, but even so, they will make their own decisions, and these decisions will be the right decisions, because they are *their* decisions. Even if there are times when we feel that they have chosen the path with the most obstacles, we must let them walk down it and learn from it, fall and get back up, turn around, and look for a better way. Even when it hurts, we must let them be free. What we CAN do is tell them our opinions and experiences, and our champions will know what to do. We must trust them, and understand that there is something to be learned from each of life's lessons, and we must let them live and experiment in order to learn, grow, and become better people each and every day.

Role of Champions' Parents

B EFORE I BEGIN, I WANT to mention that I understand that all of us, as parents, want what is best for our champions. But sometimes, this intense passion to help them backfires. I only want to help you to help your champions to be better people and athletes, and to make their dreams come true... but, not to make *your* dreams come true through *them*.

Our role as parents is, in reality, very simple and fun.

We must support them to realize their dreams. Let's remember this, as it is very important.

The best way to help them is by loving them unconditionally, and accepting them the way they are. We are just guides, that little voice in their heads that says "over here, this way!"

We need to have loving relationships with our champions. We need them to know that we are there to support them, to offer a hug when things are tough, to give them advice at the right moment, or a smile when they are feeling blue.

A sincere kiss can change their whole perspective, and some encouraging words can motivate them to keep going after their dreams. Show them your confidence and trust when they are tired, so that they can continue to forge ahead.

They need us to play that role, and if we don't do it, they will look for another person to satisfy that emotional need.

In the end, we are their parents, and they are our champions.

As an important part of our champions' development, we should be familiar with their environment: their friends, places they like to hang out, their school, social activities, etc.

This is so that we may guide them, as I have mentioned before, to a healthy lifestyle.

As parents, we need to help our champions stay motivated and focused on their dreams.

With regards to motivation, it is important to determine what kinds of rewards we will use to motivate and how we will use them. Motivation can come in many forms. We can give rewards for positive attitudes, good behavior, accomplishments, etc. And these rewards can be anything from a hug or a kiss, to spending quality time with our champions and making a space in our daily routines just for them. One thing I recommend that you avoid, except on occasion and always in a balanced way, are material items.

If you look at it this way, in reality, you can see that our champions don't really need us to do any particular things to motivate them, but rather, through our daily, loving interactions with them, our champions will always be motivated.

When we choose a golf coach and other trainers, we have already evaluated them. They have ideas and values similar to our family's. We make a decision, and we feel that these people are the best fit for our champions at the moment. At that point, we need to let our champions go, that is, we need to allow the coach and other trainers to do their jobs. After all, this is why we made the decision to hire them. If there is a particular issue or concern regarding our champions' performance, then we should have a meeting with the golf coach or other trainer, where we can discuss these concerns in detail. I recommend that the champions not be present at these meetings, unless it is strictly necessary.

Having a harmonious relationship with the golf coach and other trainers is important for the proper development of our champions. There are times when the parents want to take on roles that they aren't supposed to, as they are not experts in the field. This is a mistake, because we can take away the golf coach or other trainer's authority, and if we contradict their instructions, the only thing we are doing is causing confusion and insecurity in our champions.

We must remember that we made the decision to hire a specific person or people to train our champions, so we need to trust them and allow the learning process to take place. Give them a reasonable amount of time to see results. This can be fast in some cases, slower in others. It all depends on our champions' time investment, interest, effort and commitment.

If we decide that we need to change the golf coach or other trainers, we should remember to take our champions into account, and make sure they agree with the change, so that they stay on course.

Remember that as parents, we must demonstrate love, affection, understanding, kindness, guidance, hugs, kisses, laughter ...all positive vibrations.

ROLE OF THE GOLF COACH

Your champions' golf coach is qualified to transfer information and help them reach a higher level of learning in all golf-related aspects.

He or she needs to be the head in charge of your champions´ golf careers.

His role is very important, so he should be highly qualified, and have experience and preparation in technical aspects, golf instruction, rules and regulations, mental aspects, game strategy, etc.

He needs to be empathetic, supportive and understanding towards your champions.

The golf coach knows when to push your champions. At times, he will be the bad guy, since, as I mentioned before, parents should avoid taking on this role that they so often try to assume. The coach helps your champions become better golfers and better people, and he is in charge of what they do. The coach needs to pressure your champions in certain key moments in their lives, while at the same time offering affection and understanding.

Emotionally, the coach is an important figure; using verbal motivation, he will help your champions through decisive moments in their lives.

The coach needs to go with the champions to all or most of the tournaments where they compete, so that he can observe their attitudes and behavior during tournaments, something he can't see in the regular training sessions.

The coach is the captain of the training team with regards to golf. This means that the coach needs to identify what areas the champions need to work on, and then relay this information to the physical trainer, the nutritionist, the mental trainer, etc so that they can work with your champions on improving those areas.

This way, the golf coach has overall knowledge of the champions.

Sometimes, the golf coach plays all the roles of a training team, and in this case he is in charge of everything, including exercise and mental preparation, to guide his champions to success.

The coach also advises and makes recommendations to the parents about which tournaments to compete in, so he should be familiar with national and international tournaments, as well as with the processes and deadlines for golf scholarships in universities abroad.

He should have good communication with the parents about what's going on with their champions, so that, together, they can help when need be.

In terms of technical aspects, only the coach knows what to teach and what to "un-teach." Some techniques work well for some, but not for others. The coach identifies what works for each champion, and intensifies it. He needs to understand the champions personally, that is, to create a general technique and customize it to the individual characteristics of each champion.

I have seen some golf academies that want to teach one standard swing and apply it to all champions. This is a big mistake, since we are all unique individuals, some taller, some shorter, some more flexible in certain parts of the body than in others. Of course it is easier to teach a standard swing, since you just teach one general technique and apply it to everyone. But it isn't about what is easier for the coach, but rather, what is best for the champions.

The coach needs to continually educate himself in order to stay up to date in terms of technologies, techniques, sports psychology, golf rules, fitness and nutrition.

Personally, I have been very empathetic with my students and former students. It has come naturally for me to understand them, to put myself in their shoes according to their age, to be one of them, to love them unconditionally, to listen to them, to give them my point of view even when it is not the same as theirs (I have always said that we can agree to disagree), to respect them and to sympathize with them. We have fun together, we play around, I am myself, and yet I am a child, authentic and real. I am patient and tolerant, and I understand that we are trying to reach a common goal. I support them through hard times, they know that I am there for them for whatever they need me, not only for sports related problems. They understand the difference between when I am their friend and when I am their coach. They teach me and I teach them. I recognize that I have learned from them, as they have learned for me. I am/ we are always happy, always content.

ROLE OF THE CHAMPION

THE ROLE OF THE CHAMPION is the most important, because when they fulfill their role satisfactorily, the objectives are met. When champions become the best at something, they become their best selves, and vice versa!

All of the other roles are supporting roles; each trainer does their part to complement the role of the champion, thus forming a whole.

When the champions do their part, they are committed and responsible for their acts, and then everything flows divinely.

The role of the champions is central, if they want to, they can. It's as simple as that.

With a committed support group surrounding the champions, they become responsible and fulfill their roles with love, cheerfulness and dedication, turning into real CHAMPIONS.

Your champions also need to rest and relax; there

is a time and place for everything. But, it is important that when your champions train, they give a hundred percent, in mind, body and spirit.

They need to learn to develop their passion with a positive attitude, dedication, love, happiness, character, and kindness, in short, to stand out among the rest, to be leaders, unique and authentic. They need to learn to feel, follow and put their hearts into what they do, always focusing on helping others, and always grateful, kind, compassionate, happy and giving towards their fellow man.

ROLE OF THE CHAMPIONS' ADDITIONAL TRAINERS

FOR THOSE WHO ABLE TO have chosen to hire additional trainers, it is important to understand their specific roles. These trainers are a second line of support.

In order to form a group of trainers similar to those of professional golfers worldwide, it is important to understand the following: Imagine a circle in the middle: this is the champion. Outside of this circle, there is a larger circle, divided into two parts, with the parents or family above in one part, and the coach below in the other part. Outside of this circle, is a semicircle below the golf coach, which is divided into several parts, and represent the additional trainers, such as the nutritionist, mental trainer, manager, public relations consultant, image consultant, etc, as many as the champions need. In this case, I am referring to older champions who have a broader interest and international exposure.

All of the additional trainers need to know how to perform their jobs optimally, for example, the nutritionist develops a nutritional profile, measures the percentage of muscle mass, weight, and height, and creates a special diet for golfers. He shows the champions what to eat before, during, and after a tournament, etc. The mental trainer creates a psychological profile; hypnotherapy has generated impressive results, in fact, many professional golfers use it to improve their focus on what they REALLY want, working with positive affirmations. The physical trainer identifies the champions' physical strengths and weaknesses to develop routines to help the champions be physically balanced, as well as increase flexibility and resistance, and so on and so forth with the other trainers.

Diagram of a Champion

From this diagram shown on the opposite page, we can see how important the champions are. They are at the center of the diagram and it must be this way, because it is *their* dream we are focusing on. Remember that the rest of us are there for support. From this diagram, we can see how important it is that the other trainers report their information back to the coach, and the coach in turn, reports to the parents and champions. This way, all of the communication is focused and the door to the champions' future success is wide open.

Similarly, if the coach is unsatisfied with the performance of any of the other trainers, he must discuss this with the parents and the champions as well, in order to make a group decision that will ensure the champions' continual development.

The Purpose of a Game

U NDERSTANDING THE PURPOSE OF A game is fundamental.

Life is simple and easy, and the simpler, the better.

If we think about the purpose of a game, let's ask ourselves this simple question: How do you play a game? Well, by playing it, and *playing* is synonymous with *fun*, right?

When you see a child playing a game, what is he doing? Having fun! If you ask a child what he most likes to do, he will surely answer, PLAY. At least that's what my little teacher says to me! And why do you think they like to play? Because they have FUN! It's as clear and simple as that.

So, the purpose of a game is to have fun. If you or your champions are doing something other than having fun when you play golf, you are surely doing something wrong.

More than competing, wanting to be first at everything, letting our egos dominate, there is something more substantial, more important and real, and that is having fun. I promise that if you have fun, you will play golf well, enjoying the feeling of being in nature, having a good time, and feeling happy, and your high vibration will be contagious and you will share it with the people around you.

So, please, learn how simple and easy games are, and have fun playing them!

Remember to always think, feel and behave as we REALLY want to.

What is Winning?

WHEN I ASK MY LITTLE champion teachers this simple question, I get many different responses, all of them learned from their parents or other adults who want the best for them. When I hear their answers, I realize they are on the wrong path, and it is not surprising that very few will become true winners.

I have witnessed occasions when little teachers are extremely angry, frustrated and upset, because they felt that they didn't "win" according to the standard definition of winning.

As I have mentioned, let's focus on what we REALLY want. The definition of winning must be understood and explained as follows:

Winning: Having fun and giving it your all in a game.

That is winning. When we win, we feel good, happy, a pleasant feeling or emotion. If you have fun and have done your best in a game, it is important that you feel good, because you are a winner!

The other term for "winning," the one that most people understand, is being in first place. But that is only a place among a group of players. How can a player "win," while having a bad attitude, a short temper, and allowing himself to have negative emotions? Please, let's keep a healthy perspective.

You can win (having fun and giving your best "intentions and attention") and simultaneously be in first place. In fact, you will often find yourself in first place when you win!

I have had many experiences as a golf instructor, and I will tell you some of them later on. But for now, I would like to comment that I have seen parents who tell their champions to beat the opponent. Wait a minute! How can they make a sport that is so beautiful, educational and formative, into something so awful, so personal, so "me against you"? Golf is magical, because you play against yourself, that is, to always improve, to exceed your own limits, to be a better player each day.

Forget about the other players, play your game, and let them play theirs. Everyone has their own goals and strategies, and if you meet yours, good for you, and if the other guy meets his too, well, we should congratulate him from the heart, since he, too is evolving into a better person.

Ask the little champions why they play golf, and the majority will respond: to make friends, to see new courses, to have fun, to be outdoors, for a personal challenge, etc. All sweet, harmonious and beautiful comments.

So, here is a message we need to learn: Let's put our egos aside and simply flow with the magic of a game as wonderful as golf.

DIFFERENT AREAS
OF LEARNING

A S OUR CHAMPIONS DEVELOP /EVOLVE, it is important to know and understand the different areas of learning.

Most parents are only interested in scores, as if they had a company in which they focus on income without caring about anything else. I don't doubt that the only thing they would see in such a case would be losses! Sometimes less is more. We need to focus on the human side.

During your champions' development, there are a series of lessons to be learned one by one, which collectively will form a ladder to help each champion reach this or her own personal success, at just the right moment.

These lessons are:

- **Keep a positive attitude:** What you CAN do when facing any situation is to maintain a positive attitude. Teaching your champions to be positive, to think and behave positively, is an important lesson you can teach them. It's a way of life. It doesn't matter what the situation is, always stay positive. This teaches us to be accepting, and to understand that this is the way things are for now, and by having a positive attitude, we can learn and understand what life is trying to teach us. Remember that life gives us what we need in order to learn, grow, and be better people, and not necessarily only what we want. If we also need what we want, then it will happen.

- **Know the proper technique:** When under pressure, stress, or at a decisive moment, knowing the proper technique will help us to be victorious. It is important that the technique be fully understood, reasoned and felt physically. Your champions need to know how to perform the correct movements for each particular shot. They need to know their own bodies, the movements of each muscle in order to perform the correct technique. They need to be in good physical condition so the movements can be made correctly. When I say this, what I mean is that golf doesn't require a very strong body, but it does require a flexible one. Doing Yoga or Pilates along with eating a healthy diet will help the muscles become flexible.

- **Know the rules of the game:** When you play a game, you need to be familiar with the basic rules, otherwise, you might be the best golfer, but, because you were unaware of the rules, you would get so many penalty shots that you would turn into the world's worst golfer. It is important to know the basic rules to show respect for the game and your fellow players. As for the advanced rules, there are rules judges present during tournaments who have studied all the rules of golf.

- **Mental aspects:** Accepting and knowing yourselves mentally will help you with our internal processes. Each person is different, everyone has their own ideas, some are more explosive on the course, and others are more easy-going, and both are fine, because they have different temperaments. It is important to learn how to control yourself, though, and to be able to accept yourself throughout the game, always with the goal of finding your center, remaining calm, and at peace and in harmony with yourself. When we can do this, we can transform those negative attitudes into positive ones, which will motivate ourselves to play better and to benefit from everything that we are and that we have inside to become better people. Accepting ourselves, respecting ourselves and loving ourselves, continually transforming our weaknesses into strengths for our benefit and for the benefit of others around us.

- **Nutrition:** Champions need to know what food and drinks are the best to obtain a flexible and healthy body. What should I eat? When should I eat? What should I eat before, during and after a tournament? They need to try a variety of healthy foods and drinks and learn to listen to their bodies. Our bodies will tell us if what we are eating is good for us.

- **Exercise:** Champions need to know how to warm up before and after a tournament, what exercises improve flexibility, what are the best exercises for golf. Today, there is a lot of easily accessible information available about these topics. There are programs available on the Internet which helps us attain healthy and flexible bodies conducive to golf.

- **Scores:** Basically, if we can understand and incorporate the points mentioned above into our daily lives, then we can also have good scores, and therefore be the best scorers of a golf tournament. Everything goes hand in hand. To get good scores, we must have a positive attitude. Champions must have a good technical understanding and ability in order to make good shots. They must know the basic rules of golf in order to understand the game and its process, and to help fellow players. They need to have the right game mentality in order to perform body movements with confidence, and they need to have clear minds in order to get good scores. Good nutrition and exercise will help their mental and physical processes. And all of these together will give us trophies at the tournaments.

As you can see, there are different areas of learning, and each champion will surely have others, since each one is an individual with his or her own particular needs.

Parents need to understand that each area of learning

requires a process that takes time and adaptation. With love and patience, your champions can be better players.

Parents also need to understand the universal law of the pendulum. This law shows us how, during the Champions' processes, as in the process of life, there are ups and downs just like a pendulum, with movements that start up, then move down, then move back up again, and so forth. This is important to understand, because the champions' processes are also like this, and the down moment, in the world of sports, is called a *slump*. These *slumps* happen to all of us. Let's focus on golf and our champions: there will be times when they are successful and other times when they are less so. This is normal; it is a life process that we must accept. When our champions are in a slump, it is critical that everyone offer them their support, because this is a big factor in their ability to get out of the slump as soon as possible. How can we help them? That's easy, just by supporting them, motivating them, and talking with them about the process. Then, with unconditional love, they will come out victorious…until the next slump! Yes, because there will be another slump…it's a universal law. There are good times and others that are not so good. Once we understand and accept this, we can get out of these slumps quickly.

Every great athlete goes through this process. It is completely normal. It is up to us to help the champion get out of it. If the champions have the support of their parents, golf coach and other instructors, they can get out of the situation just like foam.

THE IMPORTANCE
OF THE WORD

A S THEIR GUIDES, WE NEED to teach our champions with our words. It is important that they be positive and that they always refer to the message we REALLY want to transmit. The message should be clear and precise, so that the instructions that we want to give remain in the champion's subconscious.

For example, if we don't want them to touch something, it is better to say, "Leave that there, it's fragile." If we don't want them to climb up on something because it is dangerous, we should say, "It's safer if you stay on the ground."

How many times have you said, "Don't scream!" and they scream more? That's why it's better to say, "Be quiet" instead.

Words have an important meaning in our subconscious, so with this simple and easy method, we can guide our little champions more successfully.

Words have an amazing effect on our conduct. Communicating proactively is a very valuable tool.

Remember that through our words, we show our champions what we REALLY want them to do.

True Stories

A T THIS POINT, I WOULD like to share with you some experiences I have had with champions and their parents.

These stories will help you to learn, through the experiences of others, about the positive and negative effects of their actions.

These stories, ranging from happy to cheerful to sad, are all true.

I have changed the names of the people who I have learned so much from through their experiences. Thanks to them, I have become a better person.

I offer a heartfelt thanks to all those who have helped me to learn these lessons.

DEMANDING PARENT

FERNANDO, 9 YEAR OLD JAIME'S father, was very demanding. Lucky for Fernando, little Jaime had an amazing ability for golf, which is why he saw a lot of potential in the little champion. Fernando demanded a lot from Jaime. He had a nutritionist, sports psychologist, physical trainer, and of course, classes with a golf instructor. There was so much pressure on Jaime that he started to play badly. Fernando felt that his champion was distracted and unmotivated, so he started to push him harder.

Jaime felt so much pressure, that he couldn't handle it. He was tired, he started getting bad grades at school, and his golf was getting worse by the day. Not only that, but he was also a lonely child, with no friends and no childhood.

One day, I saw him playing in a tournament, and I saw how Fernando was following him like a spectator, and I approached Fernando, and asked him how Jaime was doing, to which he responded that he was playing terribly, that he was missing all the shots. At that moment, Jaime teed off from the third hole on a relatively easy par four, with a wide fairway. His shot went directly out of bounds, and Fernando, who was about twenty yards away, started shouting about how he could make a shot like that, and then threw his hat on the ground and stormed off. I walked over to Jaime and told him that it was okay, that it was a game and he should have fun, which, of course, was not easy because he was stressed out from his father's reaction and plus, he was only nine.

I approached Fernando again, and told him that he should try to remember that Jaime was just a nine year old kid, and that so much pressure was not healthy. Fernando disagreed. Even so, I insisted that it would be good for Jaime to enjoy his childhood, play with toys, spend afternoons with friends, have fun and participate in other activities besides golf, and leave the psychologist, nutritionist and physical trainer until Jaime was older. Fernando said, no, that his son was a good player, and he needed to pressure him more for him to get even better.

I simply repeated that he was making a mistake from my point of view, and I left.

Three months later, I ran into Fernando at another

tournament, and I saw that Jaime was shooting the best score of his life. Fernando came up to me and thanked me. I asked him, "Thanks for what?" to which he replied that he had thought about, understood and accepted what I had said to him three months earlier. He had talked to Jaime about it, and had decided to simply let his champion be a nine year old child, with no additional trainers. Jaime is once again, a great golfer.

PROFESSIONAL GOLF
PLAYER PARENT

JACINTO WAS A PROFESSIONAL GOLF player, and his daughter, Pamela was twelve. For personal reasons, he could not give classes to his daughter, because they didn't have the best relationship at the time. So, Jacinto asked me if I would teach Pamela, and I agreed.

After a few weeks of classes, I ran into Jacino and he told me he would like to talk to me. He mentioned that his daughter was very happy, and then began suggesting some technical changes to Pamela's swing. We exchanged opinions, and then Jacinto asked me to teach Pamela some movements that I don't agree with. I explained my point of view and why I wasn't going to teach that movement to Pamela. Jacinto got angry, because he wanted Pamela to have the same swing as his, since that was the swing that he had used during his professional golf career. I explained to Jacinto that each person is different, and some are more flexible than others, that Pamela was very flexible, and a few other technical points. By the end of the conversation, Jacinto still insisted that he wanted his daughter to have his swing. So, I asked Jacinto if he had asked Pamela what she wanted: Jacinto didn't respond…he didn't know what to say. I continued and told him that I thought it would be best if we cancelled the classes, because otherwise Pamela would only be confused between my methodology and his.

Sadly, Pamela never took classes with me again. From this story, we can learn that we can't be right all the time. If things are going well, let the positive energy flow, we are a team, supportive, united and love.

KNOW-IT-ALL, EGOCENTRIC PARENT

MARIO, TEN YEAR OLD JOSE'S father, was a great golf player. He had taken several golf clinics in the United States, and he had a 2 handicap. For some reason, Mario wanted me to give classes to Jose. We began, and Jose was progressing satisfactorily; he had begun to understand the game better, and had begun to improve his golf technique. One Saturday, Mario shot a sixty-eight in the club where he played. When he finished, he came to watch his champion at the practice range, while I was giving him class. Mario arrived all big-headed, bragging to everyone that he had shot a sixty-eight, and showing his scorecard to anyone who crossed his path. He came over to me, and said, "Look, coach, I shot a sixty-eight," and I didn't pay much attention, I only glanced at him briefly to say congratulations. Mario continued on, giving me a shot by shot recap, until finally, I turned around and said, "Mario, please let me finish the class with your champion, Jose. When we are finished, we can talk all about your round." Mario half-agreed, and stood back to watch the class. A few minutes later, he came up to me and said, "Coach, tell him to make this movement that has worked well for me," and once again, I barely acknowledged him, just slightly nodding my head. Then, a few minutes after that, he came up to me again to suggest another technique. Once again, I asked him to please let me give the class to Jose, and told him that I knew that he was a great player, but that Jose needed other things for the moment.

Not surprisingly, Mario took it personally and told Jose that the class was over. Then he told me that he could give me classes whenever I wanted, and that from this moment on, he would be giving Jose classes.

And that's what happened, for a time Mario gave classes to Jose. I humbly wish them both the best.

OVERPROTECTIVE PARENT

ALICIA, EIGHT YEAR OLD ALVARO'S mother, overprotected her champion. I saw it during tournaments. In the eight to nine year old category, champions can have a caddie, so Alicia caddied Alvaro, and if it was hot, she took out an umbrella to protect him from the sun; she carried four bottles of water in case he was thirsty, etc. Alvaro, logically, grew accustomed to this treatment. And then, when he turned ten, his world changed. In the ten to eleven year old category, there were no caddies allowed, and so suddenly, Alvaro had to carry his own golf bag, umbrella, bottles of water, etc. Of course, he wasn't able to manage all that. In short, Alicia, by wanting to "help" her champion, had overprotected and in effect, spoiled him. In the end, Alvaro learned to play alone, with no umbrella for the sun, with one bottle of water, and just the basics to survive on the golf course. Was it hard for him? Yes, it was!

JEALOUS PARENT

Luis, FOURTEEN YEAR OLD ROBERTO'S father, was acting a bit strange. Robert had been taking classes with me for three years, and we had a good relationship, not just professionally, but a friendship. Robert would talk to me about his life, his girlfriends, problems at home, at school, etc.

At one point, I saw Luis at a golf tournament. During our conversation, he mentioned that his son, Roberto, told me more things than he did to him. I simply answered that there must be a reason and I asked him if he spent much quality time with his champion, Roberto, who was fourteen and going though many important stages of his life. Luis confessed that they didn't spend a lot of time together; he arrived late from work and traveled a lot.

I suggested that they spend more quality time together, even fifteen minutes at the end of the day or during breakfast before school.

Fortunately, Roberto and I are still good friends. He is a good person. Luis continues with his hectic work schedule.

LOVING PARENT

DANIELA, FIFTEEN YEAR OLD FATIMA'S mother, is a loving woman, who always says positive things. One day, it seemed as if Fatima was going to be the best scorer of the tournament. But, in the last hole, a par three, her tee shot went to the lake just in front of the green. In the end, Fatima hit six shots and ended up in second place. When the round ended, she was crying, and Daniela went up to her and gave her a big, maternal hug. That moment was frozen in time for me. That hug, which lasted seconds, seemed to last hours. Fatima smiled; that warm hug had changed her attitude in an instant. I walked over to Daniela and asked her what she had said to her champion. And she answered that she had told Fatima that she was her champion, that she would always be her champion, and that the score didn't matter, that she would always be by her side, and that she loved her. Today, Fatima is a great player at the national level, and above all, a great person.

Thank you, Daniela, for this wonderful lesson.

UNINTERESTED PARENT

SANTIAGO, THIRTEEN YEAR OLD ARMANDO'S father, is an excellent tennis player, and has played tennis his whole life. The whole family is a tennis family, but Armando had liked golf since he was little. This champion had developed great technique and passion for the sport. Armando had been in first place at several regional tournaments. One day, this great champion came up to me, and shared that he was frustrated, because his father had bought his brother a new tennis racquet with the latest technology, and his brother hadn't even been in the top five of any tennis tournament. And, Armando had had the same clubs for many years now. I told him that it's the player that matters most, and not the equipment but of course, having the best/right equipment helps.

Later that same day, by coincidence, although for me there are no coincidences, I saw Santiago after my golf classes. I asked him how his tennis was going, and he said it was going great, and that he had bought his other son a racquet with the latest technology. I took advantage of the moment to suggest that he buy Armando some clubs with newer technology, because Armando was growing and his clubs no longer fit. I also asked him to take note of his little champion's performance; he had been doing really well, and he deserved new clubs. Santiago responded that it wasn't worth it, that golf was a game for old people, and that in tennis, on the other hand, you have to run, do exercise, blah, blah. I asked him to think about it, and to realize that we were talking about his little champion, who was becoming an outstanding golf player.

Time went by, and about a month later, Santiago called me to ask my advice about which clubs he should buy for Armando. In that moment, my face lit up with a bright smile.

Experiences with Champions

- One day, I was giving class and the champions were not paying attention. They were distracted and talking about the immortality of crabs, so I decided it was time to put order and discipline. I started being stricter that day, and I told them that the next champion who spoke would have to do physical exercise, and that there had been enough talk, and that if they came to class, it was to practice and to become better golfers. The class lasted and hour and a half, and, in fact, it really was too strict. I wondered if I had pressured them too hard. When the class ended, I saw the angry face of one of my students, and I asked her gently, "What's the matter, Clara?", and she answered, "All I want right now is PEACE". How right she was!

- It was the rainy season, and the course where we

were training was soaked. There were puddles everywhere, mud, tall grass that hadn't been cut due to the rain, etc. Juan, a twelve year old champion, told me that he couldn't play in these conditions, that it was impossible! And so he didn't play that weekend, and then it was the feared Monday, golf classes. When Juan arrived, I asked him how he had played over the weekend, and he told me that he hadn't played because the course was in such bad condition. I responded, "Juan, you are making a big mistake. When you play in a tournament, it might rain and you'll have to play in those conditions. Nature is giving you the chance to practice and you don't want to. Give yourself the opportunity to practice on courses that aren't perfectly maintained. You need to learn to play on a fairway whether it be muddy, dry, wet, in bad or good condition, and in the heat, cold, rain or wind, whether you are sick or healthy, or with a physical or mental ailment. *That* will make you a complete champion."

• I always tell my champions to be honest with themselves. This is an important value, that they respect themselves in ideas and values. On one occasion, there were two champions in class who looked very tired. They were yawning and moved as if they were carrying big rocks on their shoulders. I took them aside and asked them what was wrong. They told me that they were very tired, that they had gone to bed late doing a school project, and that they also had a cold. I gathered all the champions together, and told them, "It is important to listen to your bodies, to be honest with yourselves, and to make sure that you feel well when you come to class. That way, we can practice at a hundred percent and we can improve. The next time you feel tired or sick, please, don't come to class. Call me and let me know what's going on, and don't come unless you feel one hundred percent." One champion told me that his father didn't care if he was tired or didn't feel well; he had to come to practice anyway in order to be a good player. My question to this father is, haven't you ever missed work because you were sick? Champions are human beings, too, and sometimes they are tired for a good reason, or they get sick. I was pleased when, the next day, the two champions didn't come to class and when I called to ask why, they answered, "Jorge, we are tired and we have a cold. We need to rest today, so that tomorrow we can be on hundred percent for the class." How wonderful!

- I prefer it when champions ask questions about what I am teaching them, rather than just stay quiet. This way I know that the champion is trying to understand and feel what I am teaching them.

- I was giving class for the first time to a group of six and seven year old champions, those little teachers who have taught me so many things! At one point, I told them to take out their eight iron, and they all appeared with their clubs in hand in front of me, except for one little teacher, who I saw looking through her bag. I walked over to her and said, "Carmen, where's your club?" to which she responds, "Teacher, I don't remember what *size* club you asked for." That really cracked me up.

- Another time I was with the same group, and there was a little teacher named Sandra. She was really swinging badly, she wasn't paying attention, she was swinging however she wanted, and didn't care what I told her to do. She was in her own world. I started to get frustrated and raised my voice. I told her that if she didn't want to practice, then she should leave the class and stop wasting my time. She then looked up at me with a sparkle of happiness in her eyes and such a sweet smile, that I understood at once that she was having fun! I was being too demanding with that little seven year old teacher.

- Finally, the greatest satisfaction these champions have given me is seeing the fruit of their labors, champions who have met their goals, be it getting a scholarship to study abroad, or having played successfully in a professional, national or regional tournament. I remember fondly each moment that a champion has been in first place in a national or international tournament, or has received his or her first golf trophy. It is amazing to see them reach a specific goal, to see their faces full of happiness, emotion, tears of joy, and also to see the faces of the parents as they emotionally congratulate their champions. To be there, to be part of the happiness, emotions and achievement, fills me with a gratifying feeling, full of affection, appreciation, goodness and love.

Thank you for letting me be part of your story.

With affection,
Jorge

POSITIVE AFFIRMATIONS

- I have fun playing golf

- Divinity flows through my swing

- I trust my swing and the outcome

- All is well

- If I want, I can

- I play easy and simple golf

- I accept any outcome

- I work on my patience everyday

- I trust my intuition

- My imagination provides creative solutions

- I act with humility and altruism

- I have a healthy self-esteem

- I act with harmony and love

- I choose positive thoughts

- I am tolerant of different opinions

- I act with kindness

- I am sincere and honest with myself

- I am focused on my goals

- I have fun along the way

- I am sensitive and generous

- I have will power and determination

- I am emotionally balanced

- I am relaxed, calm, and at peace

- I follow my own rhythm

- I know how to forgive myself

- I accept and love myself unconditionally

- I am open and receptive to all good.

You can contact Jorge at:

jorge.gomez@adargolf.com